KOI FISH

Everything You Need To Housing,

Feeding, Breeding, Behavior,

Habitat And Caring For Koi Fish

DON EDDIE

Table of Contents

CHAPTER ONE

INTRODUCTION

In case you realize a person who has a pond, chances are they keep multiple Koi to brighten it up.

Koi fish are some of the most common, fish to preserve in out of doors lawn ponds.

In Japan wherein they had been first bred, they are noticeably prized and are even the principle subjects of many myths and artwork.

Although they may be at once related to goldfish, it might be a big mistake to assume that they have the identical degree of care. These fish could by no means stay in a tank, they want an outside pond.

Are you preparing to open your pond to three Koi? Examine on to find out the first-rate feasible manner to take care of those suitable, long-dwelling carp.

CHAPTER TWO

LITTLE DESCRIPTION OF KOI FISH

Koi fish are decorative variations of the common carp (Cyprinus carpio). They belong to the circle of relatives Cyprinidae, which incorporates all carps and minnows.

The phrase Koi comes from the Japanese word for carp.

Preserving and breeding Koi started in 19th century Japan when farmers stored colorful specimens of the local carp of their rice gardens.

Now the maintaining and breeding of these fish is a tremendous and rewarding industry.

Lamentably, the recognition of those stunning fish has led them to end up invasive in waters all around the international.

In the wild, common carp most effective live for about twenty years due. However captive Koi can live as much as 50 years if they're cared for properly.

Common types observed in maximum outdoor ponds can be

purchased from pond and aquarium providers for everywhere among $50 and $80.

Unique types need to be bought from a breeder – those may be very highly-priced, starting from as low as $200 to as excessive as $1000+.

CHAPTER THREE

TYPICAL BEHAVIOR OF KOI FISH

Koi are very non violent fish with the intention to have interaction with the others in their faculty even as leaving that out of doors of their school on my own. They shape schools of everywhere among 5 and 15 people and will swim in beautifully coordinated formations.

Koi will visit each stage of your pond. They will swim and dart alongside the floor and center ranges and forage for herbal foods at the lowest.

In colder temperatures, they may shelter on the deeper levels of your pond. They're very lively and free-swimming fish in order to display off their vibrant shades at each opportunity.

Koi fish have a alternatively thrilling manner of looking for food. When foraging, they'll dig and burrow into the sediment to uproot plant life and munch on tasty seeds.

They eat like a vacuum, taking in massive gulps of meals and filtering out the dust and dust.

This is a rather uncommon feeding method that makes them a primary pest to freshwater ecosystems.

CHAPTER FOUR

TYPES OF KOI FISH

Koi fish can attain lengths of up to three ft – they're certainly one of the largest cyprinids and one in every of the largest fish typically saved in backyard ponds.

They normally have barbells on both facets of the jaw and feature a spherical snout and a toothless jaw for taking in gulps of prey.

Ladies are large and have rounder bodies than males. Normally, their fins are brief and rounded, with lobed caudal fins. But, positive sorts are bred for his or her long trailing fins.

Those terrific fish are available in putting colorations. They may be generally white or silver, with iridescent scales and colorful spots and markings.

These markings can be pink, gold, orange, black or even deep blue. Their actual shade and markings depend upon the sort.

Butterfly Koi Fish

Butterfly Koi (also called Dragon Koi) are named after their long pectoral and caudal fins. They're fairly prized and valuable to keepers.

This variety may be located in any of the everyday shade paperwork and is simplest set aside from others through the period of its fins.

Eastern Koi Fish

Those are the maximum commonplace Koi that you'll see in maximum ponds and water gardens.

Kohaku Japanese Koi is white with orange/purple markings. They're taken into consideration the standard range.

Tancho Koi is Kohaku Koi with an unmarried pink spot at the top of the pinnacle.

Dragon Koi Fish

The dragon can consult with two exclusive kinds of Koi. extra frequently, it's just another term for the Butterfly Koi.

The Kumonryu version is also called a Dragon Fish. that is a black and white fish with markings that trade depending at the seasons.

Black and White Koi Fish

Shiro Utsui fish are white with black spots and markings. Some have a cut up-head sample with white on one facet of the pinnacle and black on the alternative.

Matsuba Koi can be black and white as nicely; however also can have black markings over a crimson or gold frame.

Gold Koi Fish

Ogon is a fantastically prized one-shade range. An Ogon fish is entirely silver, orange or gold. Ordinary Koi with gold markings over white bodies are called Ki. Kinrin fish have stunning scales that sparkle like gold coins.

CHAPTER FIVE

KOI FISH HABITAT AND POND SITUATIONS

The Koi's wild counterpart, the not unusual carp, is native to Europe and Asia.

They stay in lakes, ponds, and streams with muddy bottoms and minimal go with the flow. Their mile observed in each temperate and tropical area and prefers water temperatures above 70°F.

It miles most lively in the dimly-hit hours at nightfall and dawn but will swim and forage throughout all hours of the day.

Replicating those conditions for your pond is not a difficult project.

Koi Fish Pond Setup

Your garden pond has to preserve temperatures between 74-86°F all year round. Within the iciness, a heating device can be had to save you any freezing. Water float is not essential, but the fish might be just satisfactory if you pick out to feature a small movement or waterfall on your pond.

The pH of your pond should be stored between 6-9. you could use overwhelmed limestone for your water can help to maintain your pH.

Your pond has to be made from concrete, with a rubber lining and muddy backside substrate.

The very best setup for Koi is a beautiful outside water garden, entire with non-invasive vegetation to be able to not damage your herbal environment.

The quality plants for a water garden consist of:

Water hyacinth

Water lilies

Cattails

Pickerels

Floating pondweed

Duckweed and extra

Many keepers plant willows and different shady, trailing bushes around their water lawn. This enables to provide extra color and cover for your fish.

Pond for koi fish

Koi need at the least 250 gallons of water. A faculty of large Koi will require up to 1,000 gallons.

Your pond must have a minimal intensity of at the least 6 ft and encompass each shallow and deeper area.

The rule of thumb of thumb with these fish is to hold 10 gallons of water for every inch of absolutely grown Koi.

This means 250 gallons of water for one adult fish.

CHAPTER SIX

KOI WITH OTHER FISHES

Goldfish are one of the excellent pond associates for Koi Fish.

In the wild, those fish live among different carp species. They can also be found alongside smaller Minnows and Killifish.

They're observed in lakes and streams which have large sport fish like Catfish, Perch, and Bass.

Koi are very non violent fish so that it will not harass or prey on the alternative fish for your pond, so there are quite loads of alternatives for stocking.

Goldfish are one of the maximum famous pond mate selections. They're comparable in shade and look and appearance stunning when they swim alongside each other.

Grass carp function high-quality tank pals and natural pruning systems for your pond – they have got a huge urge for food for flowers and will assist to trim down any flowers that might be developing out of manage.

Sunfish do very well along all varieties of carp – Redear sunfish area in particular popular desire for stocking a carp pond.

Different right pond buddies include Catfish, largemouth bass and striped bass. Be conscious that the larger game fish will require a larger pond size.

Amphibians (especially Frogs) make the quality non-fish pond associates. You can encourage the local Frogs, Salamanders, and Newts to drop by way of for a visit.

Its miles exceptional to attract frogs evidently for your pond, as opposed to stock your pond with frogs.

Frogs from puppy shops or different ponds can be wearing bacterial infections which can unfold for your fish.

You have to avoid preserving bluegill with any type of Carp. Bluegill and Carp are herbal opponents and they can be very destructive in your garden while competing for meals and assets.

Small Cyprinids categorized as nano fish must be avoided as nicely. These fish are often very aggravating in the presence of huge tank friends.

Preserving Koi Fish together

Koi are at their best while they are in a collection. They need to be kept in schools of at the least 5, and in larger ponds, you may preserve up to 15 fishes.

CHAPTER SEVEN

KOI FISH CARE

Koi are at risk of a deadly herpesvirus. Koi herpesvirus, or KHV, is a contagious virus that impacts all kinds of the commonplace carp. As soon as a fish has been infected, there may be an eighty percent threat that it's going to die from the infection.

Demise happens as fast as an afternoon or and any fish that live to tell the tale the infection come to be everlasting companies which could infect other carp inside the pond.

Signs and symptoms of KHV include respiratory difficulty, sunken eyes and crimson and white lesions at the gills. In many cases, the complete population ought to be euthanized once one fish is infected.

KHV may be averted through carefully examining the fitness of any new carp that you introduce for your pond. New fish ought to be quarantined for up to 2 weeks before you region them for your pond.

Other illnesses and parasites that have an effect on Koi fish consist of fish lice, ich, and ulcerative diseases that affect goldfish and other carp.

Watch for erratic or uncoordinated swimming, lethargy or respiration trouble. Your fish will gulp on the air if it's miles having problem breathing.

Despite the fact that these fish have a totally excessive tolerance for terrible water fine pond renovation is the maximum vital factor of care and disorder prevention.

You should easy the pond and test your filter out every 2 to 4 weeks.

CHAPTER EIGHT

KOI FISH FEED

Within the wild, those fish are regarded for his or her large appetites and feature a comparable diet to goldfish.

They may be omnivores that devour seeds and plant fabric, algae, zooplankton, and insects. They do now not prey on different fish but may additionally devour their eggs.

In a well-stocked pond, your fish will locate flora and critters to munch on. The best weight-reduction plan for them consists of a good blend of both herbal and industrial meals. They will conveniently devour algae and aquatic plants. You have to hold a great stock of algae and floating weeds for you to discourage them from uprooting the plants on your water garden.

To meet their love of zooplankton, introduce water fleas and brine shrimp in your pond. You could also supply them bugs and insect larvae purchased from an aquarium supplier or bait saves.

Any industrial ingredients you provide them need to be excessive in protein. They feed at all levels of the pond and can be given pellets in an effort to reach all depths. You may complement their diets with farm grains which includes rice and corn.

Most of the people of your Koi's vitamins will come from what they discover to your pond. You could provide them up to a few small quantities of extra pellet food per day. An automatic fish feeder set for two times an afternoon works wonders for maximum pond fish.

CHAPTER NINE

BREEDING KOI FISH

Breeding Koi fish would require a separate pond for mating and spawning.

It may be executed clearly or prompted through artificial way inclusive of hormone injections. The fish will attain sexual maturity among 2 and 5 years vintage and herbal breeding will occur within the springtime.

In a breeding pond, there need to be 2-3 males for each girl. Large, older girls are the satisfactory spawners.

To inspire herbal breeding situations, hold your breeding pond at temperatures among 64-72°F.

They ought to be fed meals high in protein and consist of both natural and industrial meals, up to 3 instances an afternoon.

Ladies will lay their eggs in your shallow-water vegetation, and the male will fertilize them as soon as they're laid. This form of external fertilization happens in lots of special species of fish.

Once the eggs are fertilized, they must be removed and positioned in an incubation tank. They'll hatch in 3 to four days.

Your new child fish will no longer seem like much. Within the larval stage, they're extraordinarily tiny and will flow via the water like zooplankton.

When they attain the fry level and lose their yolk sacs, they'll look like very tiny scale-much less fish.

Fry may be reared in an indoor tank till they reach the juvenile level. They ought to be fed larval brine shrimp and hardboiled eggs mixed with water.

Once they reach the juvenile stage, they may appearance much like miniature variations of the adult fish. They are able to then be positioned within the pond and given the equal meals that you provide the adults.

THE END

Printed in Great Britain
by Amazon

62805112R00031